TIMESAVING SERMON OUTLINES

Russell E. Spray

BAKER BOOK HOUSE
Grand Rapids, Michigan 49506

With love to our grandchildren,
Shari, Tami, and **Paul Musatics**
Darla and **Beth Smith**

Copyright 1981 by
Baker Book House Company

ISBN: 0-8010-8193-9

Ninth printing, April 1993

Printed in the United States of America

PREFACE

Timesaving Sermon Outlines are especially designed to be of assistance to busy pastors in their sermon preparation. They need only add their own introductions and illustrations. These outlines may also be helpful to teachers and group leaders.

I trust that *Timesaving Sermon Outlines* will be a blessing to those who use and hear them. May God be glorified.

Russell E. Spray

CONTENTS

1

A Successful Church

"Christ also loved the church, and gave himself for it; . . . that he might present it to himself a glorious church" (Eph. 5:25-27).

I. **A Scriptural Church**
   "All scripture is given by inspiration of God, . . . for instruction in righteousness" (II Tim. 3:16).
   A. Some churches fail because they do not accept the entire Bible as the Word of God, choosing only references compatible with their doctrine.
   B. A successful church in the sight of God is a Christ-centered church, Bible teaching, Bible believing, and Bible obeying. It carries the conviction that "all scripture is given by inspiration of God."

II. **A Serving Church**
   "If a brother or sister be . . . destitute of daily food, . . . ye give them not . . . what doth it profit?" (James 2:15-16).
   A. Many churches fail because they are self-centered. They do not reach out to assist the less fortunate but bestow their tithes and offerings upon themselves.
   B. God is pleased and brings success to churches that show concern for the needy, the suffering, and the bereaved.

III. **A Singing Church**
   "Speaking to yourselves in psalms and hymns and spiritual songs, singing and making melody in your heart to the Lord" (Eph. 5:19).
   A. Not all churches are happy churches. A drab, dull, listless, and unfriendly church leaves one with a feeling of dejection and despondency, having no desire to return.
   B. Successful churches are alive with joyful singing, friendliness, and happy anticipation. One leaves with a warm, welcomed feeling; love and joy engender a desire to return.

IV. A Soul-winning Church
"The harvest truly is plenteous, but the labourers are few"
(Matt. 9:37).
A. Many churches lack a burden and zeal for the unsaved. The members of these failing churches make little or no effort toward evangelism.
B. The Great Commission admonishes Christians to spread the gospel to every creature. Successful churches reach out to the lost with bus ministries, special services, and personal witnessing (Matt. 28:19-20).

V. A Spirit-filled Church
"And be not drunk with wine, . . . but be filled with the Spirit"
(Eph. 5:18).
A. Spiritual failure results in church failure. Affluence and social aspirations cause many churches to lose their spiritual fervor.
B. God must have first place in our lives and in our church. A scriptural church — serving, singing, soul-winning, and above all, spiritual — is a successful church.

2

Ask Yourself

"For even hereunto were ye called: because Christ also suffered for us, leaving us an example, that ye should follow his steps"
(I Peter 2:21).

I. What Would Jesus Think?
". . . think on these things" (Phil. 4:8).
A. Circumstances sometimes become perplexing and situations frustrating. You are tempted to negativism, discouragement, or possibly despondency.
B. Jesus would think positively, dwelling on those things of good report, expecting the best. Faith brings the victory (I John 5:4).

8

II. What Would Jesus Hear?

"Incline your ear, . . . hear, and your soul shall live" (Isa. 55:3).

A. Foul language, smut, and slander are commonly heard on television and radio.

B. Jesus would listen for the beneficial. He would hear the cries of the lonely, the needy, and the lost. Faith comes by hearing (Rom. 10:17).

III. What Would Jesus See?

"But mine eyes are unto thee, O God the Lord" (Ps. 141:8).

A. Many see only the faults and failures of others. Television presents scenes of lust, illicit sex, and violence, as does the movie screen.

B. Jesus would look for good in others. He would condemn sinful indulgence, lust, and violence. He would see the hurts and needs of the less fortunate and have compassion on them (Heb. 12:2).

IV. What Would Jesus Say?

"For out of the abundance of the heart the mouth speaketh" (Matt. 12:34).

A. Many talk about accumulating money and temporal pursuits. Some speak unkind and critical words.

B. Jesus would speak kindly. He would speak of eternal values, forgiveness of sins, cleansing of guilt, and the security of eternal life (Ps. 105:2).

V. What Would Jesus Do?

" . . . in every good work to do his will" (Heb. 13:21).

A. There are times when Christians do not know what to do. They face the question: Is this right or wrong?

B. Jesus would talk to His Heavenly Father about it. He would then make the right decision and do the right thing. When we ask in faith, the Holy Spirit will guide us to know and do the right thing (John 14:10).

VI. Where Would Jesus Go?

"I was glad when they said unto me, Let us go into the house of the Lord" (Ps. 122:1).

A. Many seek for pleasure. Satan offers many attractions that are harmful to the children of God.
B. Jesus would go to places where He could glorify His Father. He would attend church and witness to the lost. If we follow Christ's example, He will go with us" (Josh. 1:9).

3

Don'ts for Born-again Christians

"Therefore if any man be in Christ, he is a new creature: old things are passed away; behold, all things are become new" (II Cor. 5:17).

I. Don't Lust for Power
"Labour not for the meat which perisheth, but for that meat which endureth unto everlasting life . . ." (John 6:27).
A. Today's world is power hungry. Nations seek power to protect themselves and destroy other nations. Individuals want power to inflame their ego and control others.
B. God is omnipotent. No power compares with His power, and it is available to His children, enabling them to help the needy and witness to the unsaved.

II. Don't Listen to Profanity
"But these . . . speak evil . . . and shall utterly perish in their own corruption" (II Peter 2:12).
A. The airwaves are filled with profanity and blasphemy. Radio and television have influenced millions to resort to sinful practices.
B. Christians must dwell on the good, keeping minds and hearts filled with prayer and praise to God (II Tim. 1:13).

III. Don't Look at Pornography
"Having eyes full of adultery . . . beguiling unstable souls" (II Peter 2:14).

A. Today's world is corrupted with obscenity — nudity, lust, adultery, and homosexuality. Moral breakdown has invaded our nation, schools, churches, and homes (Gal. 5:19-20).
B. Christians must endeavor to reverse this moral decline by protests and example, by leading others to "Jesus the author and finisher of our faith" (Heb. 12:2).

IV. Don't Live in Pleasure
"Ye have lived in pleasure on the earth, and been wanton" (James 5:5).
A. Ours is a pleasure-mad generation. People are seeking to satisfy the empty longing and discontent in their lives.
B. Born-again Christians find contentment and satisfaction in Jesus Christ — peace and joy the world can never give.

V. Don't Love Your Possessions
"For the love of money is the root of all evil" (I Tim. 6:10).
A. Many are unhappy because they are obsessed with the love of money. Life's finest virtues are often sacrificed for personal gain.
B. The love of possessions often brings trouble and sorrow; loving God and giving Him first place brings peace and joy in the Holy Spirit (Luke 12:15).

4

Faith for Today

"Jesus answering saith unto them, Have faith in God" *(Mark 11:22).*

I. Pardoning Faith
"Therefore being justified by faith, we have peace with God through our Lord Jesus Christ" (Rom. 5:1).
A. Some fail to receive God's forgiveness because they feel they are too sinful. "Surely God will not forgive me," they say.

11

B. God desires that everyone be saved (II Peter 3:9). He is able and willing to forgive the vilest sinner (Isa. 1:18).

C. Repentance and faith bring God's pardon and peace (Eph. 2:8).

II. Purifying Faith

"Purifying their hearts by faith" (Acts 15:9).

A. Many Christians fail to completely surrender their lives to Christ; they hold some portion in reserve for selfish pursuits.

B. When we commit ourselves totally to Christ, giving Him first place in our lives, the Holy Spirit "purifies our hearts by faith."

C. Purifying faith brings power for service, enabling the Christian to share Christ with others (Acts 1:8).

III. Penetrating Faith

"O woman, great is thy faith: be it unto thee even as thou wilt" (Matt. 15:28).

A. There is no mountain too steep, no valley too deep for faith to handle. Faith lifts burdens, lightens bereavements, and liberates those in bondage.

B. Faith penetrates doubts, discouragements, and defeats, bringing victory to those who believe.

C. Penetrating faith is miracle-working faith. It conquers every situation and circumstance. It is the kind of faith we need for today (Mark 11:23-24).

IV. Persevering Faith

"We have access by faith into this grace wherein we stand, . . ." (Rom. 5:2)

A. Every Christian needs persevering faith when contrary winds blow and storm clouds cover the sky.

B. When there seems to be no progress, no promise, no purpose, we must just keep on keeping on — working, praying, believing; holding fast to the assurance that faith brings the victory (Acts 27:22-25).

5

How Do You Look?

"Looking unto Jesus the author and finisher of our faith" (*Heb. 12:12*).

I. **Some Look Downward**
   A. Today's news spotlights trouble and violence. Favorable reports are treated as less significant.
   B. Christians too often dwell on the dreary side of life. Pessimism brings discouragement to self, disappointment to others, and displeasure to God (Ps. 42:5, 11).

II. **Some Look Upward**
   A. The Bible admonishes God's people to look upward, in faith. God is alive; He is still on the throne and in complete control.
   B. Christians look upward because our help is from the Lord, although it may be delivered through friends, doctors, or others (Ps. 121:1).

III. **Some Look Inward**
   A. Many people in today's world are miserably unhappy because they are self-centered, concerned only about themselves.
   B. When Christians become unconcerned about the needs and salvation of others, they become dwarfed mentally and spiritually (II Cor. 5:15).

IV. **Some Look Outward**
   A. Christians should look outward with compassion and concern for the millions who without Christ are headed for eternal death and destruction.
   B. We must share Christ, leading the lost to salvation through repentance and faith (John 4:35).

13

V. Some Look Backward
  A. Some people talk about past accomplishments almost exclusively, perhaps trying to compensate for what they should be doing now.
  B. Paul gives advice to those who live in the past: "Forgetting those things which are behind . . ." Everyone can do something. Each can be a blessing if he tries (Phil. 3:13).

VI. Some Look Forward
  A. For the Christian the best is yet to come. He looks ahead with faith and anticipation, expecting to receive blessings and miracles in this life.
  B. The Christian also looks forward to the land beyond. There will be no more sin, sorrow, suffering, or separation. Look for the best. It is yet to come (Phil. 3:13-14).

6

How Satan Attacks

"Be sober, be vigilant; because your adversary the devil, as a roaring lion, walketh about, seeking whom he may devour" (I Peter 5:8).

I. Through Our Desires
"Man is tempted, when he is drawn away of his own lust, and enticed" (James 1:14).
  A. Satan attacks through legitimate as well as illegitimate desires. He attempts to drive us to extremes or to do the right things in the wrong way.
  B. We must exercise self-discipline, and through prayer, faith, and patience defeat satanic attacks. "Blessed is the man that endureth temptation: for when he is tried, he shall receive the crown of life" (James 1:12).

II. Through Our Defects

"There was given to me a thorn in the flesh, the messenger of Satan to buffet me . . ." (II Cor. 12:7).

A. Satan harassed the apostle Paul through his thorn in the flesh. Satan attacks us also through our afflictions, infirmities, and sicknesses.

B. Paul asserted: "When I am weak, then am I strong." He trusted the Lord. In our weaknesses, God's grace is sufficient for us, too. "My grace is sufficient for thee: for my strength is made perfect in weakness" (II Cor. 12:9).

III. Through Our Defeats

"For Satan himself is transformed into an angel of light" (II Cor. 11:14).

A. Everyone becomes discouraged and feels defeated at times. It is after we have floundered that Satan takes advantage of us.

B. During times of defeat we must take positive action and put our faith to work. We must reach out to help the less fortunate, visit and pray for the sick, and share Christ with others. If we do these things, we will be encouraged and Satan will be defeated. "But the God of all grace . . . make you perfect, stablish, strengthen, settle you" (I Peter 5:10).

IV. Through His Deceits

"Satan . . . shall go out to deceive the nations" (Rev. 20:7-8).

A. Satan is constantly trying to deceive and defeat God's people. He is the accuser of the brethren, beguiling them through his subtlety (II Cor. 11:3).

B. Our defense is in God. Through His love and grace we are more than conquerors (Rom. 8:37-38). Declare as Christ did, "Get thee behind me, Satan."

7

How to Glorify God

Scripture Reading: Psalm 65
"Praise waiteth for thee, O God, in Sion: and unto thee shall the
vow be performed" (Ps. 65:1).

I. **Rely on the Grace of God (Ps. 65:1-4)**
"As for our transgressions, thou shalt purge them away" (Ps. 65:3).
   A. The songwriter wrote: "Amazing grace! how sweet the sound! / That saved a wretch like me!" Forgiveness and cleansing cannot be purchased or earned. They are free gifts of God's grace (Titus 3:7).
   B. God doesn't always give us an easy way, but He does supply needed grace. The apostle Paul received sufficient grace for his thorn in the flesh (II Cor. 12:9).

II. **Recognize the Greatness of God (Ps. 65:5-8)**
"Which by his strength setteth fast the mountains; being girded with power" (Ps. 65:6).
   A. Many Christians fail to recognize the greatness of God. God's natural attributes include:
      1. omniscience — He has perfect knowledge and understanding of all things.
      2. omnipresence — His presence is everywhere.
      3. omnipotence — He can do all things because He is all-powerful.
   B. God is great in love and compassion. He lives within those who love and trust Him and supplies their needs (Phil. 4:19).

III. **Rejoice in the Goodness of God (Ps. 65:9-13)**
"The little hills rejoice on every side . . . the valleys also are covered over with corn; they shout for joy, they also sing" (Ps. 65:12-13).

A. Failure to praise the Lord and rejoice in His goodness indicates a selfish life.
B. God forgives and cleanses those who come to Him. He heals the afflicted, comforts the bereaved, lifts the fallen, and loves the unloveable.
C. God so greatly loved us that He gave His only begotten Son to die for our sins. He deserves our praise and we glorify Him when we rejoice in His goodness.

8

How to Handle Hurts

"Beloved, think it not strange concerning the fiery trial which is to try you, as though some strange thing happened unto you' (I Peter 4:12).

I. **Consider the Source**
"Rejoice, inasmuch as ye are partakers of Christ's sufferings" (I Peter 4:13).
A. Consider the source of offenses. Some hurt others because of ignorance or frustration, possibly originating in an unfortunate childhood. Others deliberately and maliciously injure others because of satanic dominion in their lives.
B. Consider *your* source — God is the Christian's fount of strength. Understanding and compassion will often heal your hurt. Pray earnestly for and forgive your offender.

II. **Consider the Spirit**
"If ye be reproached for the name of Christ, happy are ye, . . . he is glorified" (I Peter 4:14).
A. Consider the spirit of those who hurt you. Many hurt others unintentionally, unaware of the impact of their words or actions. Contrarily, some try to lift their self-esteem by putting another down, or hurt others to get even.

B. Consider *your* spirit. Always give others the benefit of the doubt. If someone hurts you without intent and awareness, then quickly forgive and forget. If the injury was deliberate, pray for your offender. Forgive him. Love him. Remember it is his problem; don't make it yours. Keep a good spirit — God's Holy Spirit.

III. **Consider the Solace**
"If any man suffer as a Christian, let him not be ashamed; . . . glorify God" (I Peter 4:16).
A. There is no solace from God for those who deliberately and maliciously injure His children. He will make recompense.
B. Consider your solace: "God is our refuge and strength, a very present help in trouble" (Ps. 46:1). Continue to love, forgive, and pray for those who despitefully use you. God is your solace, and you are conquerors through Him. "Casting all your care upon him; for he careth for you" (I Peter 5:7).

9

It's Time for a Change

"And be not conformed to this world: but be ye transformed by the renewing of your mind . . ." (Rom. 12:2).

I. **God Has Formed**
"God formed man of the dust of the ground, . . . and man became a living soul" (Gen. 2:7).
A. "In the beginning God created the heaven and the earth" (Gen. 1:1). "God formed every beast of the field, and every fowl of the air" (Gen. 2:19).
B. Mankind was the crown of God's creation. "God created man in his own image, . . . male and female . . ." (Gen. 1:27). He was given dominion over all God's creation — beast, fish, and fowl (Gen. 1:28).

II. Sin Has Deformed

"For the wages of sin is death" (Rom. 6:23).

A. Man was removed from the Garden of Eden because of his disobedience to God. Sin marred man's image and brought sorrow, suffering, and death to the human race.

B. Jesus Christ, the perfect Lamb of God, died for all the sins of the human race (Gal. 5:19-21).

III. Religion Has Reformed

"Having a form of godliness, but denying the power thereof" (II Tim. 3:5).

A. True religion is based on Bible principles, which cannot be improved. God's Word is the authority on theology, philosophy, and psychology.

B. Religion that offers reform alone falls short of its real potential and purpose. The saving, cleansing, redemptive power of Jesus Christ is the basis for truly effective religion.

IV. Education Has Informed

"Ever learning, and never able to come to the knowledge of the truth" (II Tim. 3:7).

A. We live in the most educated society in history. Scientific achievements and medical discoveries have made tremendous contributions to our world. But mankind is still frustrated and searching for fulfillment.

B. Education can meet our mental and physical needs, but to meet our spiritual needs we must be changed by a spiritual birth.

V. Jesus Christ Can Transform

"If any man be in Christ, he is a new creature: old things are passed away . . . all things are become new" (II Cor. 5:17).

A. According to Webster, to transform means "to change in nature, disposition, heart . . . convert." That's exactly what Jesus Christ does for those who come to Him.

B. When we repent of our sins and believe, we are forgiven. As we commit our lives totally to Christ, He cleanses and fills us with God's divine love.

C. Have you been transformed? If not, it is time for a change! (Gal. 5:22-24).

10

Jesus Christ the Way

"Jesus saith unto him, I am the way . . ." (John 14:6).

I. The Way to Pardon
"If we confess our sins, he is faithful and just to forgive us our sins. . . ." (I John 1:9).
  A. Because of Adam's fall, all mankind is marred by sin. Each becomes accountable for his own sins.
  B. To be released from the guilt of sin, one must receive pardon. No kings, presidents or angels can forgive the sins of man.
  C. Jesus Christ paid the penalty for our sins by His death on the cross. He alone is the way to pardon for all who repent and believe (Col. 1:14).

II. The Way to Purity
". . . the blood of Jesus Christ his Son cleanseth us from all sin" (I John 1:7).
  A. Many Christians fail to completely surrender their lives to Jesus Christ, but hold back some portion for themselves.
  B. Only as we yield to Jesus Christ in total commitment can we be cleansed from all sin and filled with His divine love.
  C. Jesus Christ is the way to purity of heart; He shed His blood so we could be reconciled to God (I John 1:9).

III. The Way to Peace
"Peace I leave with you, my peace I give unto you" (John 14:27).
  A. There is less peace today than ever before. Our world is filled with hatred, strife, self-seeking, separation, and divorce.
  B. Millions are searching for peace through self-effort, education, psychology, and the accumulation of material possessions.
  C. Jesus Christ is the only way to lasting peace — real peace.

When we turn our lives over to Him in total commitment, He takes over the responsibility and gives us peace (Phil. 4:7).

IV. **The Way to Power**
"I can do all things through Christ which strengtheneth me" (Phil. 4:13).
A. Men and nations seek power to dominate and destroy one another.
B. Christians seek power to assist the less fortunate and bring the lost to a saving knowledge of Jesus Christ.
C. Jesus Christ is the way to power. His Holy Spirit empowers consecrated Christians to do God's work (Acts 1:8).

11

Surrounded by God

"As the mountains are round about Jerusalem, so the Lord is round about his people from henceforth even for ever" (Ps. 125:2).

I. **Surrounded by God's Promises**
"Whereby are given unto us exceeding great and precious promises: that by these ye might be partakers of the divine nature . . ." (II Peter 1:4).
A. By believing and accepting God's promises, we receive His presence.
B. We receive cleansing and are filled with the Holy Spirit when we commit our lives totally to God; we are partakers of His divine nature (I John 2:25).

II. **Surrounded by God's Peace**
"And the peace of God, which passeth all understanding, shall keep your hearts and minds through Christ Jesus" (Phil. 4:7).
A. Millions are searching for peace in our troubled world. In

education, psychology, medicine, weapons, and war they find only disappointment and frustration.

B. There is no real and lasting peace outside of God. When Christians encounter troubles, testings, and trials, they rely on the peace of God. This holds them steady through the tempest (John 14:27).

III. Surrounded by God's Protection

"For he shall give his angels charge over thee, to keep thee in all thy ways. They shall bear thee up in their hands . . ." (Ps. 91:11-12).

A. Ours is a dangerous world, unsafe by night and day. Many people change locations, hoping to find safety from the violence produced by man and nature.

B. In God's hands, Christians who are totally committed to His will are safe and secure. God surrounds His children with His protective care while they do the work He wants them to do.

C. When the Christian's life work is finished, God has reserved a home in heaven for him where there is eternal safety (John 14:1-3).

IV. Surrounded by God's Power

"Who are kept by the power of God through faith unto salvation ready to be revealed in the last time" (I Peter 1:5).

A. Nations seek for the power to control or destroy other nations. Some individuals want power to dominate other people. This kind of power is satanic and self-defeating.

B. God's power is greater than Satan's power. Christians are kept by God's power, conquerors through Him.

C. The Holy Spirit empowers Christians for service: to help the needy, pray for the sick, comfort the bereaved, and witness to the unsaved (Acts 1:8).

12

Power of the Gospel

"For I am not ashamed of the gospel of Christ: for it is the power of God unto salvation to every one that believeth" (Rom. 1:16).

I. **Power for Salvation**
   "If we confess our sins, he is faithful and just to forgive us our sins, and to cleanse us from all unrighteousness" (I John 1:9).
   A. Man has made great strides, but none of his achievements can bring forgiveness and cleansing to his own heart and soul.
   B. The Gospel is the power of God to bring salvation to all mankind.
   C. When we surrender to God in total commitment, the Holy Spirit cleanses and fills us with the love of God.

II. **Power for Serenity**
   "And the peace of God, which passeth all understanding, shall keep your hearts and minds through Christ Jesus" (Phil. 4:7).
   A. All of man's amazing scientific achievements have failed to bring peace. There are more strifes, more conflicts, and wars than ever before.
   B. The only source of real and lasting peace today is found in the power of the gospel.
   C. When we accept Jesus Christ as Saviour and Lord of our life, we may claim the promise, "The peace of God . . . shall keep your hearts and minds through Christ Jesus" (Phil. 4:7).

III. **Power for Security**
   "To an inheritance . . . reserved in heaven for you, who are kept by the power of God through faith . . ." (I Peter 1:4-5).
   A. Millions are searching for security through education, popularity, and the accumulation of wealth.
   B. The only real and lasting source of security is found in the gospel of Jesus Christ.

C. Earth's treasures wear out, rust, and decay. The love of God, salvation, and the assurance of eternal life are forever. They are lasting and eternal.

IV. **Power for Service**
"But ye shall receive power, after that the Holy Ghost is come upon you: and ye shall be witnesses unto me . . ." (Acts 1:8).
A. Many Christians are weak, faltering, lacking in courage, concern, and power to do God's work.
B. When Christians make a total commitment to God, they are cleansed and filled with the Holy Spirit.
C. Surrendered Christians are empowered by the Holy Spirit, enabling them to work, witness, and win the lost to Jesus Christ (Acts 1:8).

13

Take Time for God

"But seek ye first the kingdom of God, and his righteousness; and all these things shall be added unto you" (Matt. 6:33).

I. **Ponder His Word**
"Thy word have I hid in mine heart, that I might not sin against thee" (Ps. 119:11).
A. Many Christians neglect the Word of God. They may read a few verses hurriedly but fail to take the time to ponder them as they should.
B. God has fellowship with His children and gives them direction through His Word. We must respond by taking time to meditate on His word (Ps. 119:47-48).

II. **Practice His Ways**
"And he will teach us of his ways, and we will walk in his paths" (Isa. 2:3).
A. In today's world many practice the ways of Satan more than

24

the ways of God. They are self-centered, inconsiderate of others, unforgiving, and filled with hostility and hate.

B. We should be kind, helpful, understanding, forgiving, and filled with God's love. In giving God first place in our lives, we will be "practicing His ways" (Isa. 45:13).

III. **Possess His Will**

" . . . that ye may stand perfect and complete in all the will of God" (Col. 4:12).

A. Christians sometimes have difficulty concerning God's will in certain areas of their lives, stubbornly clinging to their own desires.

B. God has first place in our lives only when we surrender everything to Him, committing our will totally to His will. "Trust also in him; and he shall bring it to pass" (Ps. 37:5; see also Eph. 6:6).

IV. **Participate in His Work**

"I must work . . . while it is day: the night cometh, when no man can work" (John 9:4).

A. Failure to participate in God's work is evidence of lukewarmness and lack of concern.

B. We must take time for God by becoming involved in His Kingdom, being faithful in church attendance, and participating in the work of the church.

C. We should share Christ with the unsaved, urging them to repent of their sins and confess Christ as Saviour and Lord (Matt. 9:37-38).

14

Take Time for Others

"And be ye kind one to another, tenderhearted, forgiving one another, even as God for Christ's sake hath forgiven you" (Eph. 4:32).

I. **Be Considerate of Others**
   "Put on . . . mercies, kindness, humbleness . . . Forbearing . . . and forgiving one another . . . " (Col. 3:12-13).
   A. Those who disregard the feelings and rights of others are often the first to complain when their own accomplishments go unnoticed.
   B. Take time to consider the feelings, regard the rights, and notice the accomplishments of others. This is essential to growth in Christ (II Cor. 5:14-15).

II. **Be Concerned About Others**
   "But whoso hath this world's goods, and seeth his brother have need, and shutteth up his bowels of compassion from him, how dwelleth the love of God in him?" (I John 3:17).
   A. Too many people are self-centered, overly concerned with their pains, problems, and personal pursuits, caring only about themselves.
   B. We must feel concern for the needy and the unsaved, have compassion on the afflicted, and comfort the bereaved. We are blessed as we take time for God and others. Let us . . . love . . . in deed and in truth" (I John 3:18).

III. **Be Cooperative with Others**
   "For we are labourers together with God . . ." (I Cor. 3:9).
   A. Many families and churches are like a team of horses pulling in opposite directions. Only confusion can be accomplished under those circumstances.
   B. We must work together in unity and harmony, asking God for direction, working together with Him. In this manner the Lord's work will be accomplished successfully (II Cor. 6:1).

IV. Be Christlike Toward Others

"And walk in love, as Christ hath also loved us, and hath given himself for us . . ." (Eph. 5:2).

A. Much unhappiness among Christians is caused by the holding of resentments. See Romans 12:10.

B. Totally committed Christians are victorious. Forgiven, cleansed, and filled with God's love, they are "kind one to another, tenderhearted, forgiving one another, even as God for Christ's sake hath forgiven" them (Eph. 4:32).

15

Take Time to Live

"For what is your life? It is even a vapour, that appeareth for a little time, and then vanisheth away" (James 4:14).

Many spend their lives seeking personal gain. They fail to achieve the things that are most rewarding. They need to:

I. Take Time to Listen

"Incline your ear, and come unto me: hear, and your soul shall live" (Isa. 55:3).

A. Listen to others. Everyone needs a listening ear at times. Listening encourages, solves problems, brings comfort and healing to the brokenhearted and bereaved.

B. Listen to God. We receive help from Him when we hear and heed His council; we receive His care and comfort when we take time to listen (Ps. 91:15).

II. Take Time to Learn

"Thy word is a lamp unto my feet, and a light unto my path" (Ps. 119:105).

A. Learn from God. By reading and meditating on God's Word, through prayer and faith, we receive wisdom from above (Ps. 119:133).

B. Learn from people. We can learn much from the knowledge and experience of others. Good books, papers, and newscasts are learning sources.

III. Take Time to Laugh

"A merry heart doeth good like a medicine" (Prov. 17:22).

A. Many Christians do not take time to laugh. Their lives are dreary and drab.

B. We should learn to laugh at ourselves, enjoy others, and rejoice in the Lord. Counting our blessings and praising God for them enables us to be happy Christians (Ps. 126:2).

IV. Take Time to Lift

"But Jesus took him by the hand, and lifted him up" (Mark 9:27).

A. Jesus forgave sin, gave sight to the blind, healed the sick, raised the dead. He took time to lift.

B. Many are too busy with personal pursuits and pleasures to lift the less fortunate. As Jesus took time for others, so must we.

V. Take Time to Love

"God is love; and he that dwelleth in love dwelleth in God, and God in him" (I John 4:16).

A. To take time to love is to take time for God, since God is love. Everyone needs to share in the love of God.

B. We take time to live by sharing God's love — a smile, a kind word, a helping hand, and sharing Christ (I John 4:21).

16

The H-A-N-D-S of Jesus

*"Jesus knowing that the Father had given all things into his hands
. . ." (John 13:3).*

I. **H-ealing Hands**
"And he touched her hand, and the fever left her" (Matt. 8:15).
   A. The power of God was released and the sick and afflicted
   were healed when Jesus touched them (Matt. 8:3).
   B. The touch of the Master's hand releases God's power today.
   His healing power is actuated through prayer and faith.

II. **A-nointing Hands**
"And he took them up in his arms, put his hands upon them,
and blessed them" (Mark 10:16).
   A. Children are symbolic of humility. When they were brought
   to Jesus, He touched them and blessed them. Jesus placed
   special blessings upon those who came to Him in humility
   and faith.
   B. Jesus honors the humble. Those who totally commit
   themselves to Him He anoints with power and blessing.

III. **N-ail Pierced Hands**
"Reach hither thy finger, and behold my hands; . . . Thomas
answered . . . My Lord and my God" (John 20:27-28).
   A. When Jesus was crucified, His hands were nailed to the cross;
   He suffered and died a cruel death for our sins.
   B. The nail-pierced hands of Jesus represent His love and
   sacrifice, which made it possible for all to receive forgiveness
   and cleansing.

IV. **D-edicated Hands**
"But Jesus took him by the hand, and lifted him up" (Mark
9:27).
   A. The hands of Jesus are dedicated hands. As He listens to
   those in distress, He loves and lifts (Mark 6:2).

B. We should also have dedicated hands. We follow Christ's example by helping the less fortunate, lifting their burdens, and sharing Christ with the unsaved.

V. S-aving Hands

"Behold, I stand at the door, and knock" (Rev. 3:20).

A. Many have used their hands to bless others and to save lives.
B. Christ alone can save souls. He patiently and lovingly knocks at the door of every heart. Open the door and let Him come in.

17

The Importance of Faith

"But without faith it is impossible to please him: for he that cometh to God must believe that he is, and that he is a rewarder of them that diligently seek him" (Heb. 11:6).

I. Faith Brings Salvation

"For by grace are ye saved through faith" (Eph. 2:8).

A. When a sinner repents with godly sorrow and believes God's promises, he receives forgiveness of sins.
B. When the Christian totally commits his life to Jesus Christ, he receives cleansing and is filled with the Holy Spirit (Rom. 10:9-10).

II. Faith Gives Serenity

"My peace I give unto you: not as the world giveth, give I unto you" (John 14:27).

A. The world today seeks peace through education, psychology, doctors, and medicines. In spite of the help these afford, there is more unrest and turmoil than ever before.
B. The only real and lasting peace is found in Jesus Christ. We cannot earn or buy it. We have only to accept it by faith. "My peave I *give* unto you."

III. Faith Affords Security
"O the depth of the riches both of the wisdom and knowledge of God!" (Rom. 11:33).
- A. Many are striving for security through temporal pursuits — accumulating money, investments in real estate, etc.
- B. True security is found only in Jesus Christ. Earthly treasures wear out, rust, and deteriorate. The riches that Christ affords are eternal; the life He gives is everlasting (Eph. 2:7).

IV. Faith Requires Service
"Even so faith, if it hath not works, is dead, being alone" (James 2:17).
- A. Many Christians are less than victorious because they fail in the service department — to God and man.
- B. Service for God is faith in action. Faith brings salvation, serenity, and security — and requires service.
- C. When we help the needy, visit the sick, comfort the bereaved, and witness to the lost, we exhibit a living faith necessary to victorious living (James 2:18-26).

18

The Lord Is G-R-E-A-T

"For thou are great, and doest wondrous things: thou art God alone" (Ps. 86:10).

I. Great G-od
"Thou shewest lovingkindness unto thousands . . . the Great, the Mighty God . . ." (Jer. 32:18).
- A. God is omnipotent — all-powerful. "There is nothing too hard for thee" (Jer. 32:17).

B. God is omniscient. He is all-wise, having knowledge of everything (Acts 15:18).
C. God is omnipresent (Ps. 139:7). God is immutable; He is unchangeable (Mal. 3:6; Heb. 13:8).
D. God is eternal — from everlasting to everlasting (Rev. 1:8). The Lord is a great God.

II. Great R-edeemer
"Who gave himself for us, that he might redeem us from all iniquity . . ." (Titus 2:14).
A. To redeem means "to regain possession by payment of amount due." Through disobedience man estranged himself from God. Sin brought the sentence of death upon the human race.
B. No good works, sacrifice, or money could purchase redemption; neither kings nor angels could atone for sin.
C. Only the perfect Son of God could bring redemption to mankind by His death on the cross.

III. Great E-mancipator
"If the Son therefore shall make you free, ye shall be free indeed" (John 8:36).
A. Moses led the children of Israel from Egypt's bondage. He was an emancipator.
B. Abraham Lincoln freed the slaves in the United States. He was an emancipator.
C. Jesus Christ freed millions of people bound by the fetters of sin. All who come to Him through repentance and faith are released from sin's bondage (John 8:32).

IV. Great A-dvocate
"And if any man sin, we have an advocate with the Father, Jesus Christ the righteous" (I John 2:1).
A. An advocate is one who pleads the cause of another.
B. Lawyers often help victims of crime and circumstances by pleading their cause in court.
C. Jesus Christ pleads the cause of Christians before God, whose mercy endures forever. He will forgive and cleanse those who believe, repent, and surrender to Jesus, our great advocate.

V. Great T-ransformer

"We shall not all sleep, but we shall all be changed, . . . and the dead shall be raised incorruptible . . ." (I Cor. 15:51-52).

A. To transform means "to change the nature, disposition, heart; convert."

B. Christians are transformed now. Old values pass away and all things become new as we approach life with the mind of Christ.

C. The best is yet to come. We shall be changed into Christ's likeness and be with Him in a land that is fairer than day. There will be no more sin, sorrow, suffering, or separation (I Cor. 15:53-58).

19

The Victory of F-A-I-T-H

"For whatsoever is born of God overcometh the world: and this is the victory that overcometh the world, even our faith" (I John 5:4).

I. F-reedom in Christ

"If the Son therefore shall make you free, ye shall be free indeed" (John 8:36).

A. Some Christians fail to enjoy their freedom in Christ. They are in bondage to circumstances, themselves, and others. Victory is available through faith.

B. Faith and repentance bring forgiveness and cleansing. Accepting Christ as Saviour and Lord brings freedom and victory, enabling one to "overcome the world" (John 8:32).

II. A-ssurance from Christ

"Be not afraid, only believe" (Mark 5:36).

A. Many Christians are dwarfed and defeated, overwhelmed by doubts and fears because of failure to accept the assurance that comes only from Christ.

B. We can trust the Lord without reservation, confident that He is able to handle everything that comes into our lives (Jude 24).

III. **I-nvolvement for Christ**

"The harvest truly is plenteous, but the labourers are few" (Matt. 9:37).

A. "I" stands for "Involvement for Christ" and is the center of the word *faith*. Failure at this point means losing the victory of "freedom" and "assurance" and the blessings to come.

B. The victory of faith includes working for Christ, for "faith without works is dead" (James 2:17). We must share Christ with the unsaved, bringing them to a knowledge of salvation (Matt. 9:38).

IV. **T-riumph Through Christ**

"We are more than conquerors through him that loved us" (Rom. 8:37).

A. Many Christians live beneath their privileges. Lack of faith brings disappointment to self, discouragement to others, and displeasure to God (Heb. 11:6).

B. Faith enables the Christian to triumph through Christ. No mountain is too steep, no valley too deep, no burden too heavy, no problem too difficult for Christ to handle (Rom. 8:38-39).

V. **H-eaven with Christ**

"I go to prepare a place for you . . . that where I am, there ye may be also" (John 14:2-3).

A. Faith is good to live by. It brings freedom, assurance, and triumph. Faith is also good to die by. Heaven awaits those who keep the faith.

B. The Christian's climactic victory of faith is eternal life, peace, and love, with no more sin, sorrow, or suffering (John 14:1-6).

20

The Voice of Jesus

"This is my beloved Son, in whom I am well pleased; hear ye him"
(Matt. 17:5).

I. **The Voice of Jesus Condemns**
"For by thy words thou shalt be justified, and by thy words thou shalt be condemned" (Matt. 12:37).
  A. Careless words may offend; they may cause souls to be lost. Loving words can give comfort and hope; they may lead souls to Christ.
  B. Jesus always spoke the right words at the right time. He condemned sin and taught love for God and man. Sinners are convicted by Christ's words concerning love and hate, life and death, and heaven and hell.

II. **The Voice of Jesus Converts**
"Son, be of good cheer; thy sins be forgiven thee" (Matt. 9:2).
  A. No earthly authority of church or state can forgive the sins of mankind.
  B. When we believe on the Lord Jesus Christ and repent of our sins, He reaches down into the gutter, lifts us out of the miry clay, and declares, "Thy sins be forgiven thee."

III. **The Voice of Jesus Cleanses**
"Jesus . . . touched him, saying. I will; be thou clean. . . . his leprosy was cleansed" (Matt. 8:3).
  A. A leper threw himself upon the mercy of Jesus, believing that He could cure him, and Jesus cleansed him of his loathsome disease.
  B. Jesus sent His Holy Spirit to cleanse and fill with God's love all Christians who totally commit their lives to Him. He is still saying, "I will; be thou clean" (John 17:16-17).

IV. The Voice of Jesus Comforts

"Jesus spake unto them, saying, Be of good cheer; it is I; be not afraid" (Matt. 14:27).

A. The disciples were storm-driven, in danger, and afraid. "The ship was now in the midst of the sea, tossed with waves: for the wind was contrary" (Matt. 14:24).

B. Christians are often tossed with waves, torn by the contrary winds of affliction and despair. Jesus is passing by — let us touch the hem of His garment. He is still saying, "Be of good comfort, thy faith hath made thee whole" (Matt. 9:22).

V. The Voice of Jesus Conquers

"I am he that liveth and was dead; and, behold, I am alive for evermore . . ." (Rev. 1:18).

A. There is power in the voice of Jesus. God spoke the universe, the earth, the land and the seas into existence. Jesus' voice conquers sin, sorrow, suffering, separation, and speaks eternal life to those who serve Him.

B. Christ is more than a match for Satan. We are conquerors through Him. He speaks victory, not only for this life, but for the world to come. Jesus is still saying, "Because I live, ye shall live also" (John 14:19).

21

T-R-U-S-T

"Trust in the Lord with all thine heart; and lean not unto thine own understanding" (Prov. 3:5).

I. T-urn to the Lord

". . . that they should repent and turn to God, . . ." (Acts 26:20).

A. Many would like to receive the benefits of trust without turning to God; to continue in sin and enjoy God's blessings, too. This is not possible.

B. We must turn from our wicked ways to the ways of the Lord. When we believe and repent, He forgives us and blesses bountifully as we trust Him (Acts 26:18).

II. R-ely on the Lord

"Commit thy way unto the Lord; trust also in him" (Ps. 37:5).

A. Some Christians do not rely on the Lord as much as they should. They depend on their own strength, financial gain, and the wisdom of others.

B. We should trust in the Lord before all else. When we put God first in our lives, we may rest assured that our needs will be supplied (Matt. 6:33).

III. U-nite with the Lord

". . . the love wherewith thou hast loved me may be in them, and I in them" (John 17:26).

A. When the Holy Spirit cleanses us and fills us with God's love, we are then one with the Lord. His presence will abide with us forever (John 17:21).

B. Surrendered Christians trust the Lord daily for peace, purity, and purpose. The Holy Spirit empowers them for service (Acts 1:8).

IV. S-erve for the Lord

"Trust in the Lord and do good" (Ps. 37:3), "for ye serve the Lord Christ" (Col. 3:24).

A. Christians too busily engaged in personal pursuits will work for possessions, pleasure, and popularity, but fall short in their service for God.

B. God must have first place in our lives. We can fully trust Him only as we reach out to others: the needy, the discouraged, the lost.

V. T-riumph in the Lord

"And the Lord shall help them, and deliver them: . . . because they trust in him" (Ps. 37:40).

A. Those who trust in the Lord — turn to Him, rely on Him, unite with Him, and serve for Him — shall also triumph in Him.

B. Not only are they victorious here and now, but they will triumph in the world to come. "They shall reign for ever and ever" (Rev. 22:5).

22

Trusting the Lord Effectively

"Trust in the Lord with all thine heart; and lean not unto thine own understanding" (Prov. 3:5).

I. **Trust Him About the Yesterdays (The Past)**
   "I . . . am he that blotteth out thy transgressions . . . and will not remember thy sins" (Isa. 43:25).
   A. Many people are laden down with guilt about the past. Their sins, mistakes, and blunders continue to haunt them. Some Christians are bothered by false guilts, too.
   B. Some may question, "Is there help for the past? Can what has been done be redone or undone?"
   C. Yes, God can forgive the past and remove the guilt. Traumatic experiences may be surrendered to God. God does not always remove the results of past living, but He can change us.
   D. When we totally commit our doubts, fears, guilts and hostilities to God, He cleanses and fills us with His love. We are enabled to trust Him about our yesterdays.

II. **Trust Him for Today (The Present)**
   "Give us this day our daily bread" (Matt. 6:11).
   A. Today is all we have. Yesterday is past and tomorrow may never come. Let us not borrow trouble from either, but simply live a day at a time.
   B. On their journey through the wilderness, the Israelites needed food. The Lord supplied them with manna from heaven. It was to be gathered fresh each day — one day at a time.
   C. On their journey through life, Christians need a fresh supply of spiritual food each day. This is received through prayer, Bible reading, and sharing Christ with others.
   D. Trust the Lord for today — live today, be happy today, love God and others today. "This is the day which the Lord hath made; we will rejoice and be glad in it" (Ps. 118:24).

III. **Trust Him with the Tomorrows (The Future)**
"I will go before thee, and make the crooked places straight"
(Isa. 45:2).
   A. Many people worry about the future. They are uncertain
   about the tomorrows and fearful of the unknown. In today's
   world of violence and strife, many face the future with fear,
   frustration, and perhaps fatalism.
   B. Christians, we must face the future with faith. "The just
   shall live by faith" (Rom. 1:17). Trust the Lord with the
   tomorrows; the responsibility belongs to Him. He is depend-
   able, able to carry our burdens (I Peter 5:7).
   C. We trust the Lord effectively about the yesterdays, the to-
   days, and the tomorrows when we lean on, rely on, and are
   confident in Him. Be assured that He is working everything
   for our good and His glory (Rom. 8:28).

23

Victory in Jesus

*"But thanks be to God, which giveth us the victory through our
Lord Jesus Christ" (I Cor. 15:57).*

I. **Prove His Promises**
". . . being fully persuaded that, what he had promised, he was
able also to perform" (Rom. 4:21)
   A. All Christians believe God's promises, but many do not
   make use of them. They live beneath their privilege and are
   less than victorious.
   B. The promises of God become effective only as we prove
   them. The more we recognize the miracles of God, the more
   He will continue to perform them for us. "If ye shall ask any
   thing in my name, I will do it" (John 14:14).

II. Practice His Presence
"For he hath said, I will never leave thee, nor forsake thee" (Heb. 13:5).

A. Some Christians hurriedly say, "Now I lay me down to sleep" type of prayers. Failing to recognize God's presence throughout the day, they live in spiritual defeat.

B. Victorious Christians practice the presence of God. They live in a spirit of prayer and fellowship with the Divine.

C. Christians who practice God's presence enjoy the warmth and comfort of the abiding Holy Spirit (John 14:18).

III. Promote His Purpose
"And ye know that he was manifested to take away our sins; and in him is no sin" (I John 3:5).

A. Christians will lack victory in Jesus when they fail to work for God. Too busy with their own pursuits, they give God no opportunity to work in their lives.

B. We must give God first place in our lives. We do this by taking time to help the needy, to visit and to pray for the afflicted, and to share the forgiveness and cleansing that Christ offers the unsaved.

C. We attain victory when we promote "the eternal purpose which he purposed in Christ Jesus our Lord" (Eph. 3:11).

IV. Proclaim His Praises
"His praise shall continually be in my mouth" (Ps. 34:1).

A. Too many Christians fail to adequately proclaim the praises of God. They take His blessings for granted.

B. Victorious Christians are praising Christians. The more we appreciate and praise God for His blessings the more blessings He bestows.

C. Praise pleases God — He is worthy of all praise. Let us praise Him more. "From the rising of the sun unto the going down of the same the Lord's name is to be praised" (Ps. 113:3).

24

What to Do with Your Faith

"Let us hold fast the profession of our faith without wavering; (for he is faithful that promised)" (Heb. 10:23).

I. **Realize the Value of Faith**
   "Above all, taking the shield of faith . . ." (Eph. 6:16).
   A. Faith is of utmost importance. Without faith we not only displease God but we can receive nothing from Him (James 1:6-7).
   B. Faith in Christ brings salvation to the repentant (Eph. 2:8), healing to the afflicted, and comfort to the bereaved.
   C. Faith brings strength, safety, security. Its value is beyond estimation (Heb. 11:6).

II. **Recognize the Vision of Faith**
   "Looking unto Jesus the author and finisher of our faith" (Heb. 12:2).
   A. "Without a vision the people perish." Many Christians want to "see" results, receiving first and believing later. They lack the vision of faith.
   B. We must keep a positive outlook. Believe (for financial, physical, mental, or spiritual needs) and we shall receive.
   C. The vision of faith brings "the evidence of things not seen" (Heb. 11:1).

III. **Radiate the Virtues of Faith**
   "Now the God of hope fill you with all joy and peace in believing . . ." (Rom. 15:13).
   A. The virtues of faith include salvation, serenity, strength, security, and joyful service unto God.
   B. We radiate the virtues of faith when we help the less fortunate, visit the sick, comfort the bereaved, and witness to the unsaved.
   C. "Rejoice with joy unspeakable." Miracles happen when we use and exercise our faith (I Peter 1:8-9).

IV. Rejoice in the Victory of Faith
"This is the victory . . . even our faith" (I John 5:4).
  A. Let us never fail to praise and glorify God when victory comes (Heb. 13:15).
  B. Rejoicing over victories of faith strengthens our faith. Sharing our victories with others inspires and increases their faith also.

25

When You Don't Know What to Do

"After that ye have suffered a while, (He shall) make you perfect, stablish, strengthen, settle you" (I Peter 5:10).

I. Try Being Patient
"Cast not away therefore your confidence. . . . For ye have need of patience. . . ." (Heb. 10:35-36).
  A. People who do not know what to do often make rash decisions and rush into actions which later bring regret and disappointment.
  B. When we are unsure about what steps to take, we should exercise patience. We should delay making important decisions or taking actions that could change the direction of our lives (James 1:3-4).

II. Try Being Prayerful
"In every thing by prayer . . . let your requests be made known unto God" (Phil. 4:6).
  A. Many people fail to pray as they should. They become so engulfed in trying to decide what to do that they fail to ask God for His guidance.
  B. If we are to come to a right decision, we must ask God, listen to God, obey God, and await God's time. When we don't know what to do, we must "pray without ceasing" (I Thess. 5:17).

III. Try Being Positive

"Whatsoever things are of good report; . . . think on these things" (Phil. 4:8).

A. Not knowing what to do often brings discouragement and self-pity.

B. We must keep an optimistic outlook. We must believe God is still on the throne and able to direct our lives.

C. Positive thinking engenders faith and confidence. "Greater is he that is in you, than he that is in the world" (I John 4:4).

IV. Try Being Productive

"Let us not love in word, neither in tongue; but in deed and in truth" (I John 3:18).

A. We should be patient, awaiting God's time and way. But we should not sit with folded hands and idle away the time.

B. Someone has said, "The secret of patience is doing something else in the meantime."

C. When you don't know what to do, do something for God. Lend a helping hand to the less fortunate and share Christ with the unsaved. This will work wonders in bringing direction and meaning to your life (I John 3:17).

26

Y-E-S, God

"For all the promises of God in him are yea, and in him Amen, unto the glory of God by us" (II Cor. 1:20).

I. Y-ield to God

"Yield yourselves unto God . . ." (Rom. 6:13).

A. Some Christians want God's will for their lives, but are unwilling to yield everything to Him.

B. "Yes, God" — means total commitment to God's entire will.

C. There must be no reservation when it comes to surrendering our will to God's will.
   1. In our private life — secret prayer, devotion, deeds, and attitudes.
   2. In our public life — all we do and say has an effect and influence on others.
D. Yielding to God is the first step toward successful Christian living (Rom. 6:16).

II. **E-ndure for God**
"Thou therefore endure hardness, as a good soldier of Jesus Christ" (II Tim. 2:3).
A. There may be those who have yielded themselves to God, but when the storm is raging and the battle comes full blast, they lack the stamina to endure.
B. Christians are subject to testing, trial, and tribulation; but God has a purpose in what He allows to come to them (Rom. 8:28).
C. Determination is necessary for endurance. "Yes, God" means to keep on keeping on regardless of situations or circumstances.
D. Patience is also necessary if we are to endure for God. We must wait in faith and happy expectation for God's way and will to be done (James 5:11).

III. **S-erve with God**
"We then, as workers together with him . . ." (II Cor. 6:1).
A. Some may willingly yield themselves to God and even endure for Him, yet fail to do God's work.
B. Some fail because of complacency. They lack concern. Others fail because of inferiority feelings. They lack confidence and courage.
C. We must trust God for concern and courage to be "workers together with Him."
D. The value of one soul is beyond estimation. "Yes, God" means working with God to bring souls to Jesus Christ. We are not alone. He goes with us (I Cor. 3:9).

27

You Can Win over Worry

"Be careful for nothing; but in every thing by prayer and supplication with thanksgiving let your requests be made known unto God" (Phil. 4:6).

I. By Dedication to God
"Whether we live therefore, or die, we are the Lord's" (Rom. 14:8).
- A. Dedicated Christians do not neglect their prayer lives, fail to study the Bible, or falter in church attendance.
- B. Devotion to the things of God brings release from self and selfish concerns. Dedication, plus God's assistance, helps us win over worry (Rom. 12:1).

II. By Dependence on God
"Commit thy way unto the Lord; . . . and he shall bring it to pass" (Ps. 37:5).
- A. Too many Christians depend solely on their own weak, finite powers. This invariably results in frustration and failure.
- B. As we surrender our will and weaknesses to God's perfect will and infinite power, He is able to carry the responsibility for our life, freeing us from excessive care and concern (Prov. 3:5-6).

III. By Delighting in God
"Rejoice in the Lord alway: and again I say, Rejoice" (Phil. 4:4).
- A. Worry dispels the Christian's delight in the Lord.
- B. We win over worry when we count our blessings and discount our losses, look for the good, overlook the bad, forgive ourselves, and forgive others (Ps. 37:4).

IV. **By Diligence for God**

"For the love of Christ constraineth us" (II Cor. 5:14).

A. When it comes to doing God's work, some Christians are unconcerned. Some are just lazy. In either case, these Christians are unhappy and unfulfilled.

B. Busy Christians are happy Christians. When we work for God, we forget about our own difficulties. The Lord cares for those who give Him first place in their lives (Col. 3:23-24).

V. **By Direction from God**

"Howbeit, when he, the Spirit of truth, is come, he will guide you into all truth" (John 16:13).

A. Many Christians are looking for direction for their lives. They rightfully want their lives to be meaningful and purposeful.

B. When we make a total commitment of our lives to God, we can stand on His promise that "he will guide you into all truth." Worry has no place in the life directed by God (Prov. 3:6).